GOOD
CITIZENSHIP

GROVER CLEVELAND (1837–1908)

GOOD CITIZENSHIP

BY
GROVER CLEVELAND

APPLEWOOD BOOKS
CARLISLE, MASSACHUSETTS

Good Citizenship was originally published by
H. Altemus of Philadelphia in 1908.

Thank you for purchasing an Applewood Book.
Applewood reprints America's lively classics—
books from the past that are still of interest to
modern readers. For a free copy of our current
catalog, write to: Applewood Books, 1 River Road,
Carlisle, MA 01741.

ISBN 978-1-55709-432-2

Printed and bound in the USA.

10 9 8 7 6 5 4 3 2

Library of Congress Cataloging-in-Publication Data
Cleveland, Grover, 1837–1908.
  Good citizenship / by Grover Cleveland.
    p.   cm.
  Originally published: Philadelphia: H. Altemus, 1908.
  ISBN 978-1-55709-432-2
1. Citizenship—United States.   2. Patriotism—
United States.   3. Holidays—United States.   I. Title.
JK1759.C636   1996
323.6 '0973–dc20   96-24915
                                              CIP

INTRODUCTION

I T is not of the author's own motion that the following essays are given to the public in this form. With characteristic modesty, Mr. Cleveland was willing that these addresses should lie undiscovered and unread in the limbo of pigeonholes or of yellowing newspaper-file; and yet the thoughtful reader will be the first to proclaim that these utterances are neither insignificant nor ephemeral. Their very themes are age-old. Before Rome was, Patriotism and Good Citizenship were the purest and loftiest ideals of the ancient world; and, through the ages that have followed, those nations have been noblest, bravest and most enduring in which love of home and love of country have been most deep-seated.

Mr. Cleveland's address on Good Citizenship was delivered before the Commercial Club of Chicago in October, 1903; and that on Patriotism and Holiday Observance before the Union League Club, of the same city, on Washington's Birthday, 1907.

GOOD CITIZENSHIP

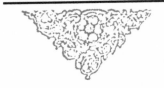

THERE is a danger that my subject of American good citizenship is so familiar and so trite as to lack interest. This does not necessarily result from a want of appreciation of the importance of good citizenship, nor from a denial of the duty resting upon every American to be a good citizen. There is, however, abroad in our land a self-satisfied and perfunctory notion that we do all that is required of us in this direction when we make profession of our faith in the creed of good citizenship and abstain from the commission of palpably unpatriotic sins.

We ought not to be badgered and annoyed by the preaching and exhortation of a restless, troublesome set of men, who continually urge upon us the duty of active and affirmative participation in public affairs. Why should we be charged with neglect of political obligations? We go to the polls on election day, when not too busy with other things, and vote the ticket our party managers have prepared for us. Sometimes, when conditions grow to be so bad politically that a revival or stirring-up becomes necessary, a goodly number of us actually devote considerable time and effort to better the situation. Of course, we cannot do this always, because we must not neglect money-getting and the promotion of great enterprises, which, as everybody knows, are the evidence of a nation's prosperity and influence.

It seems to me that within our citizenship there are many whose disposition and characteristics very often resemble those found in the membership of our churches. In this membership there is a considerable proportion composed of those who, having made profession of their faith and joined the church, appear to think their duty done when they live honestly, attend worship regularly, and contribute liberally to church support. In complacent satisfaction, and certain of their respectability, they do not care to hear sermonizing concerning the sinfulness of human nature, or the wrath to come; and if haply they are sometimes roused by the truths of vital Christianity, they soon relapse again to their tranquil and easy condition of listlessness. A description of these, found in the Holy Writ, may fitly apply to many in the State as well as in the church:

"For if any be a hearer of the word, and not a doer, he is like unto a man beholding his natural face in a glass: for he beholdeth himself, and goeth his way, and straightway forgetteth what manner of man he was."

There is an habitual associate of civic American indifference and listlessness, which reënforces their malign tendencies and adds tremendously to the dangers that threaten our body politic. This associate plays the *role* of smooth, insinuating confidence operator and, clothed in the garb of immutable faith in the invulnerability of our national greatness, it invites our admiring gaze to the flight of the American eagle, and assures us that no tempestuous weather can ever tire his wings. Thus many good and honest men are approached through their patriotic trust in our free institutions and immense national resources, and are insidiously led to a condition of mind which will not permit them to harbor the uncomfortable thought that any omission on their part can check American progress or endanger our country's continued development. Have we not lived as a nation more than a century; and have we not exhibited growth and achievement in every direction that discredit all parallels in history? After us the deluge. Why then need we bestir ourselves, and why disturb ourselves with public affairs?

Those of our citizens who are deluded by these notions, and who allow themselves to be brought to such a frame of mind, may well be reminded of the good old lady who was wont to impressively declare that she had always noticed if she lived until the first of March she lived all the rest of the year. It is quite likely she built a theory upon this experience which induced her with the passing of each of these fateful days to defy coughs, colds and consumption and the attacks of germs and microbes in a million forms. However this may be, we know that with no design or intention on her part, there came a first day of March which passed without her earthly notice.

The withdrawal of wholesome sentiment and patriotic activity from political action on the part of those who are indifferent to their duty, or foolhardy in their optimism, opens the way for a ruthless and unrelenting enemy of our free institutions. The abandonment of our country's watch-towers by those who should be on guard, and the slumber of the sentinels who should never sleep, directly invite the stealthy approach and the pillage and loot of the forces of selfishness and greed. These baleful enemies of patriotic effort will lurk everywhere as long as human nature remains unregenerate; but nowhere in the world can they create such desolations as in free America, and nowhere can they so cruelly destroy man's highest and best aspirations for self-government.

It is useless for us to blink at the fact that our scheme of government is based upon a close interdependence of interest and purpose among those who make up the body of our people. Let us be honest with ourselves. If our nation was built too much upon sentiment, and if the rules of patriotism and benignity that were followed in the construction have proved too impractical, let us frankly admit it. But if love of country, equal opportunity and genuine brotherhood in citizenship are worth the pains and trials that gave them birth, and if we still believe them to be worth preservation and that they have the inherent vigor and beneficence to make our republic lasting and our people happy, let us strongly hold them in love and devotion. Then it shall be given us to plainly see that nothing is more unfriendly to the motives that underlie our national edifice than the selfishness and cupidity that look upon freedom and law and order only as to many agencies in aid of their designs.

Our government was made by patriotic, unselfish, sober-minded men for the control or protection of a patriotic, unselfish and sober-minded people. It is suited to such a people; but for those who are selfish, corrupt and unpatriotic it is the worst government on earth. It is so constructed that it needs for its successful operation the constant care and guiding hand of the people's abiding faith and love, and not only is this unremitting guidance necessary to keep our national mechanism true to its work, but the faith and love which prompt it are the best safeguards against selfish citizenship.

Give to our people something that will concentrate their common affection and solicitous care, and let them be their country's good; give them a purpose that stimulates them to unite in lofty endeavor, and let that purpose be a demonstration of the sufficiency and beneficence of our popular rule, and we shall find that in their political thought there will be no place for the suggestions of sordidness and pelf.

Who will say that this is now our happy condition? Is not our public life saturated with the indecent demands of selfishness? More than this, can any of us doubt the existence of still more odious and detestable evils which, with steady, cankering growth, are more directly than all others threatening our safety and national life? I speak of the corruption of our suffrage, open and notorious, of the buying and selling of political places for money, the purchase of political favors and privileges, and the traffic in official duty for personal gain. These things are confessedly common. Every intelligent man knows that they have grown from small beginnings until they have reached frightful proportions of malevolence; and yet respectable citizens by the thousands have looked on with perfect calmness, and with hypocritical cant have declared they are not politicians, or with silly pretensions of faith in our strength and luck have languidly claimed that the country was prosperous, equal to any emergency and proof against all dangers.

Resulting from these conditions in a manner not difficult to trace, wholesome national sentiment is threatened with utter perversion. All sorts of misconceptions pervade the public thought, and jealousies, rapidly taking on the complexion of class hatred, are found in every corner of the land. A new meaning has been given to national prosperity. With a hardihood that savors of insolence, an old pretext, which has preceded the doom of ancient experiments in popular vote, is daily and hourly dinned in our ears. We are told that the national splendor we have built upon the showy ventures of speculative wealth is a badge of our success. Unsharing contentment is enjoined upon the masses of our people, and they are invited, in the bare subsistence of their scanty homes, to patriotically rejoice in their country's prosperity.

This is too unsubstantial an enjoyment of benefits to satisfy those who have been taught American equality, and thus has arisen, by a perfectly natural process, a dissatisfied insistence upon a better distribution of the results of our vaunted prosperity. We now see its worst manifestation in the apparently incorrigible dislocation of the proper relations between labor and capital. This of itself is sufficiently distressing; but thoughtful men are not without dread of sadder developments yet to come.

There has also grown up among our people a disregard for the restraints of law and a disposition to evade its limitations, while querulous strictures concerning the actions of our courts tend to undermine popular faith in the course of justice, and, last but by no means least, complaints of imaginary or exaggerated shortcomings in our financial policies furnish an excuse for the flippant exploitation of all sorts of monetary nostrums.

I hasten to give assurance that I have not spoken in a spirit of gloomy pessimism. I have faith that the awakening is forthcoming, and on this faith I build a cheerful hope for the healing of all the wounds inflicted in slumber and neglect.

It is true that there should be an end of self-satisfied gratification, or pretense of virtue, in the phrase, "I am not a politician," and it is time to forbid the prostitution of the word to a sinister

use. Every citizen should be politician enough
to bring himself within the true meaning of the
term, as one who concerns himself with "the
regulation or government of a nation or State for
the preservation of its safety, peace and prosperity."
This is politics in its best sense, and this is good
citizenship.

If good men are to interfere to make political
action what it should be, they must not suppose
they will come upon an open field unoccupied by
an opposing force. On the ground they neglected
they will find a host of those who engage in
politics for personal ends and selfish purposes,
and this ground cannot be taken without a hand-
to-hand conflict. The attack must be made under
the banner of disinterested good citizenship, by
soldiers drilled in lessons of patriotism. They must
be enlisted for life and constantly on duty.

Their creed should bind together in generous
coöperation all who are willing to fight to make
our government what the fathers intended it
to be—a depository of benefits which, in equal
current and volume, should flow out to all the
people. This creed should teach the wickedness of

attempting to make free opportunity the occasion
for seizing especial advantages, and should warn
against the danger of ruthless rapacity. It should
deprecate ostentation and extravagance in the life
of our people, and demand in the management
of public affairs simplicity and strict economy.
It should teach toleration in all things save
dishonesty and infidelity to public trusts.

It should insist that our finance and currency
concern not alone the large traders, merchants
and bankers of our land, but that they are
intimately and every day related to the well-being
of our people in all conditions of life, and that,
therefore, if any adjustments are necessary they
should be made in such manner as shall certainly
maintain the soundness of our people's earnings
and the security of their savings. It should enjoin
respect for the law as the quality that cements the
fabric of organized society and makes possible a
government by the people. And in every sentence
and every line of this creed of good citizenship
the lesson should be taught that our country is a
beautiful and productive field to be cultivated by
loyal Americans, who, with weapons near at hand,

whether they sow and reap or whether they rest, will always be prepared to resist those who attempt to despoil by day and pilfer in the night.

In the day when all shadows shall have passed away and when good citizenship shall have made sure the safety, permanence and happiness of our nation, how small will appear the strifes of selfishness in our civic life, and how petty will seem the machinations of degraded politics.

There shall be set over against them in that time a reverent sense of coöperation in Heaven's plans for our people's greatness, and the joyous pride of standing among those who, in the comradeship of American good citizenship, have so protected and defended our heritage of self-government that our treasures are safe in the citadel of patriotism, "where neither moth nor rust doth corrupt, and where thieves do not break through nor steal."

PATRIOTISM
AND HOLIDAY
OBSERVANCE

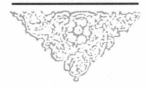

THE American people are but little given to the observance of public holidays. This statement cannot be disposed of by the allegation that our national history is too brief to allow the accumulation of days deserving civic commemoration. Though it is true that our life as a people, according to the standard measuring the existence of nations, has been a short one, it has been filled with glorious achievements; and, though it must be conceded that is not given to us to see in the magnifying mirage of antiquity the exaggerated forms of American heroes, yet in the bright and normal light shed upon our beginning and growth are seen grand and heroic men who have won imperishable honor and deserve our everlasting remembrance. We cannot, therefore, excuse a lack of commemorative inclination and a

languid interest in recalling the notable incidents
of our country's past under the plea of a lack of
commemorative material; nor can we in this way
explain our neglect adequately to observe days
which have actually been set apart for the especial
manifestation of our loving appreciation of the
lives and the deeds of Americans who, in crises
of our birth and development, have sublimely
wrought and nobly endured.

If we are inclined to look for other excuses,
one may occur to us which, though by no means
satisfying, may appear to gain a somewhat fanciful
plausibility by reason of its reference to the law of
heredity. It rests upon the theory that those who
secured for American nationality its first foothold,
and watched over its weak infancy were so
engrossed with the persistent and unescapable
labors that pressed upon them, and that their
hopes and aspirations led them so constantly to
thoughts of the future, that retrospection nearly
became with them an extinct faculty, and that thus
it may have happened that exclusive absorption in
things pertaining to the present and future became
so embedded in their natures as to constitute

a trait of character descendible to their posterity, even to the present generation. The toleration of this theory leads to the suggestion that an inheritance of disposition has made it difficult for the generation of today to resist the temptation inordinately to strive for immediate material advantages, to the exclusion of the wholesome sentiment that recalls the high achievements and noble lives which have illumined our national career. Some support is given to this suggestion by the concession, which we cannot escape, that there is abroad in our land an inclination to use to the point of abuse the opportunities of personal betterment, given under a scheme of rule which permits the greatest individual liberty, and interposes the least hindrance to individual acquisition; and that in the pursuit of this we are apt to carry in our minds, if not upon our lips, the legend:

"Things done are won; joy's soul lies in the doing."

But the question is whether all this accounts for our indifference to the proper observance of public holidays which deserve observance.

There is another reason which might be advanced in mitigation of our lack of commemorative enthusiasm, which is so related to our pride of Americanism that, if we could be certain of its sufficiency, we would gladly accept it as conclusive. It has to do with the underlying qualities and motives of our free institutions. Those institutions had their birth and nurture in unselfish patriotism and unreserved consecration; and, by a decree of fate beyond recall or change, their perpetuity and beneficence are conditioned on the constant devotion and single-hearted loyalty of those to whom their blessings are vouchsafed. It would be a joy if we could know that all the bright incidents in our history were so much in the expected order of events, and that patriotism and loving service are so familiar in our present surroundings, and so clear in their manifestation, as to dull the edge of their especial commendation. If the utmost of patriotism and unselfish devotion in the promotion of our national interests have always been and still remain universal, there would hardly be need of their commemoration.

But, after all, why should we attempt to delude ourselves? I am confident that I voice your convictions when I say that no play of ingenuity and no amount of special pleading can frame an absolutely creditable excuse for our remissness in appropriate holiday observance.

You will notice that I use the words "holiday observance." I have not in mind merely the selection or appointment of days which have been thought worthy of celebration. Such an appointment or selection is easy, and very frequently it is the outcome of a perfunctory concession to apparent propriety, or of a transient movement of affectionate sentiment. But I speak of the observance of holidays, and such holidays as not only have a substantial right to exist, but which ought to have a lasting hold upon the sentiment of our people—days which, as often as they recur, should stimulate in the hearts of our countrymen a grateful recognition of what God has done for mankind, and especially for the American nation; days which stir our consciences and sensibilities with promptings to unselfish and unadulterated love of country; days which warm and invigorate our devotion to the supreme ideals which gave life to our institutions and their only protection against death and decay. I speak of holidays which demand observance by our people in spirit and in truth.

The commemoration of the day on which American independence was born has been allowed to lose much of its significance as a reminder of Providential favor and of the inflexible patriotism of the fathers of the republic, and has nearly degenerated into a revel of senseless noise and aimless explosion, leaving in its train far more of mishap and accident than lessons of good citizenship or pride of country. The observance of Thanksgiving Day is kept alive through its annual designation by Federal and State authority. But it is worth our while to inquire whether its original meaning, as a day of united praise and gratitude to God for the blessings bestowed upon us as a people and as individuals, is not smothered in feasting and social indulgence. We, in common with Christian nations everywhere, celebrate Christmas, but how much less as a day commemorating the birth of the Redeemer of mankind than as a day of hilarity and the interchange of gifts.

I will not, without decided protest, be accused of antagonizing or deprecating lighthearted mirth and jollity. On the contrary, I am an earnest advocate of every kind of sane, decent, social enjoyment, and all sorts of recreation. But, nevertheless, I feel that the allowance of an incongruous possession by them of our commemorative days is evidence of a certain condition, and is symptomatic of a popular tendency, which are by no means reassuring.

On the days these words are written, a prominent and widely read newspaper contains a communication in regard to the observance of the birthday of the late President McKinley. Its tone plainly indicates that the patriotic society which has for its primary purpose the promotion of this particular commemoration recognizes the need of a revival of interest in the observance of all other memorial days, and it announces that "its broader object is to instil into the hearts and minds of the people a desire for real, patriotic observance of all of our national days."

Beyond all doubt, the commemorations of the birth of American heroes and statesmen who have rendered redemptive service to their country in emergencies of peace and war should be rescued from entire neglect and from fitful and dislocated remembrance. And, while it would be more gratifying to be assured that throughout our country there was such a spontaneous appreciation of this need, that in no part of our domain would there be a necessity of urging such commemorations by self-constituted organizations, yet it is comforting to know that, in the midst of prevailing apathy, there are those among us who have determined that the memory of the events and lives we should commemorate shall not be smothered in the dust and smoke of sordidness, nor crushed out by ruthless materialism.

On this day the Union League Club of Chicago should especially rejoice in the consciousness of patriotic accomplishment; and on this day, of all others, every one of its members should regard his membership as a badge of honor. Whatever else the organization may have done, it has justified its existence, and earned the applause of those whose love of country is still unclouded, by the work it has done for the deliverance of Washington's birthday from neglect or indolent remembrance. I deem it a great privilege to be allowed to participate with the League in a commemoration so exactly designed, not only to remind those of mature years of the duty exacted by their heirship in American free institutions, but to teach children the inestimable value of those institutions, to inspire them to emulation of the virtues in which our nation had its birth, and to lead them to know the nobility of patriotic citizenship. The palpable and immediate good growing out of the commemorations which for twenty years have occurred under the auspices of the League are less impressive than the assurance that, in generations yet to come, the seed thus sown in the hearts of children and youth will bear the fruit of disinterested love of country and saving steadfastness to our national mission.

In furtherance of the high endeavor of your organization, it would have been impossible to select for observance any other civic holiday having as broad and fitting a significance as this. It memorializes the birth of one whose glorious deeds are transcendently above all others recorded in our national annals; and, in memorializing the birth of Washington, it commemorates the incarnation of all the virtues and all the ideals that made our nationality possible, and gave it promise of growth and strength. It is a holiday that belongs exclusively to the American people. All that Washington did was bound up in our national life, and became interwoven with the warp of our national destiny. The battles he fought were fought for American liberty, and the victories he won gave us national independence. His example of unselfish consecration and lofty patriotism made manifest, as in an open book, that those virtues were conditions not more vital to our nation's beginning than to its development and durability. His faith in God, and the fortitude of his faith, taught those for whom he wrought that the surest strength of nations comes from the support of God's almighty arm. His universal and unaffected sympathy with those in every sphere of American life, his thorough knowledge of existing American conditions, and his wonderful foresight of conditions yet to be, coupled with his powerful influence in the councils of those who were to make or mar the fate of an infant nation, made him a tremendous factor in the construction and adoption of the constitutional chart by which the course of the newly launched republic could be safely sailed. And it was he who first took the helm, and demonstrated, for the guidance of all who might succeed him, how and in what spirit and intent the responsibilities of our chief magistracy should be discharged.

If your observance of this day were intended to make more secure the immortal fame of Washington, or to add to the strength and beauty of his imperishable monument built upon a nation's affectionate remembrance, your purpose would be useless. Washington has no need of you. But in every moment, from the time he drew his sword in the cause of American independence to this hour, living or dead, the American people have needed him. It is not important now, nor will it be in all the coming years, to remind our countrymen that Washington has lived, and that his achievements in his country's service are above all praise. But it is important—and more important now than ever before—that they should clearly apprehend and adequately value the virtues and ideals of which he was the embodiment, and that they should realize how essential to our safety and perpetuity are the consecration and patriotism which he exemplified. The American people need today the example and teachings of Washington no less than those who fashioned our nation needed his labors and guidance; and only so far as we commemorate his birth with a sincere recognition of this need can our commemoration be useful to the present generation.

It is, therefore, above all things, absolutely essential to an appropriately commemorative condition of mind that there should be no toleration of even the shade of a thought that what Washington did and said and wrote, in aid of the young American republic have become in the least outworn, or that in these later days of material advance and development they may be merely pleasantly recalled with a sort of affectionate veneration, and with a kind of indulgent and loftily courteous concession of the value of Washington's example and precepts. These constitute the richest of all our crown jewels; and, if we disregard them or depreciate their value, we shall be no better than "the base Indian who threw a pearl away richer than all his tribe."

They are full of stimulation to do grand and noble things, and full of lessons enjoining loyal adherence to public duty. But they teach nothing more impressive and nothing more needful by way of recalling our countrymen to a faith which has become somewhat faint and obscured than the necessity to national beneficence and the people's happiness of the homely, simple, personal virtues that grow and thrive in the hearts of men who, with high intent, illustrate the goodness there is in human nature.

Three months before his inauguration as first President of the republic which he had done so much to create, Washington wrote a letter to Lafayette, his warm friend and Revolutionary ally, in which he expressed his unremitting desire to establish a general system of policy which, if pursued, would "ensure permanent felicity to the commonwealth"; and he added these words:

"I think I see a path as clear and as direct as a ray of light, which leads to the attainment of that object. Nothing but harmony, honesty, industry and frugality is necessary to make us a great and happy people. Happily, the present posture of affairs, and the prevailing disposition of my countrymen promise to coöperate in establishing those four great and essential pillars of public felicity."

It is impossible for us to be in accord with the spirit which should pervade this occasion if we fail to realize the momentous import of this declaration, and if we doubt its conclusiveness or its application to any stage of our national life, we are not in sympathy with a proper and improving observance of the birthday of George Washington.

Such considerations as these suggest the thought that this is a time for honest self-examination. The question presses upon us with a demand for reply that will not be denied:

Who among us all, if our hearts are purged of misleading impulses and our minds freed from perverting pride, can be sure that to-day the posture of affairs and the prevailing disposition of our countrymen coöperate in the establishment and promotion of harmony, honesty, industry and frugality?

When Washington wrote that nothing but these was necessary to make us a great and happy people, he had in mind the harmony of American brotherhood and unenvious good-will, the honesty that insures against the betrayal of public trust and hates devious ways and conscienceless practices, the industry that recognizes in faithful work and intelligent endeavor abundant promise of well-earned competence and provident accumulation, and the frugality which outlaws waste and extravagant display as plunderers of thrift and promoters of covetous discontent.

The self-examination invited by this day's commemoration will be incomplete and superficial if we are not thereby forced to the confession that there are signs of the times which indicate a weakness and relaxation of our hold upon these saving virtues. When thus forewarned, it is the height of recreancy for us obstinately to close our eyes to the needs of the situation, and refuse admission to the thought that evil can overtake us. If we are to deserve security, and make good our claim to sensible, patriotic Americanism, we will carefully and dutifully take our bearings, and discover, if we can, how far wind and tide have carried us away from safe waters.

If we find that the wickedness of destructive agitators and the selfish depravity of demagogues have stirred up discontent and strife where there should be peace and harmony, and have arrayed against each other interests which should dwell together in hearty coöperation; if we find that the old standards of sturdy, uncompromising American honesty have become so corroded and weakened by a sordid atmosphere that our people are hardly startled by crime in high places and shameful betrayals of trust everywhere; if we find a sadly prevalent disposition among us to turn from the highway of honorable industry into shorter crossroads leading to irresponsible and worthless ease; if we find that widespread wastefulness and extravagance have discredited the wholesome frugality which was once the pride of American-ism we should recall Washington's admonition that harmony, industry and frugality are "essential pillars of public felicity," and forthwith endeavor to change our course.

To neglect this is not only to neglect the admonition of Washington, but to miss or neglect the conditions which our self-examination has made plain to us. These conditions demand something more from us than warmth and zest in the tribute we pay to Washington, and something more even than acceptance of his teachings, however reverent our acceptance may be.

The sooner we reach a state of mind which keeps constantly before us, as a living, active, impelling force, the truth that our people, good or bad, harmonious or with daggers drawn, honest or unscrupulous, industrious or idle, constitute the source of our nation's temperament and health, and that the traits and faults of our people must necessarily give quality and color to our national behavior, the sooner we shall appreciate the importance of protecting this source from unwholesome contamination. And the sooner all of us honestly acknowledge this to be an individual duty that cannot be shifted or evaded, and the more thoroughly we purge ourselves from influences that hinder its conscientious performance, the sooner will our country be regenerated and made secure by the saving power of good citizenship.

It is our habit to affiliate with political parties. Happily, the strength and solidity of our institutions can safely withstand the utmost freedom and activity of political discussion so far as it involves the adoption of governmental policies or the enforcement of good administration. But they cannot withstand the frenzy of hate which seeks, under the guise of political earnestness, to blot out American brotherhood, and cunningly to persuade our people that a crusade of envy and malice is no more than a zealous insistence upon their manhood rights.

Political parties are exceedingly human; and they more easily fall before temptation than individuals, by so much as partisan success is the law of their life, and because their responsibility is impersonal. It is easily recalled that political organizations have been quite willing to utilize gusts of popular prejudice and resentment; and I believe they have been known, as a matter of shrewd management, to encourage voters to hope for some measure of relief from economic abuses, and yet to "stand pat" on the day appointed for realization.

We have fallen upon a time when it behooves every thoughtful citizen, whose political beliefs are based on reason and who cares enough for his manliness and duty to save them from barter, to realize that the organization of the party of his choice needs watching, and that at times it is not amiss critically to observe its direction and tendency. This certainly ought to result in our country's gain; and it is only partisan impudence that condemns a member of a political party who, on proper occasion, submits its conduct and the loyalty to principle of its leaders to a Court of Review, over which his conscience, his reason and his political understanding preside.

I protest that I have not spoken in a spirit of pessimism. I have and enjoy my full share of the pride and exultation which our country's material advancement so fully justifies. Its limitless resources, its astonishing growth, its unapproachable industrial development and its irrepressible inventive genius have made it the wonder of the centuries. Nevertheless, these things do not complete the story of a people truly great. Our country is infinitely more than a domain affording to those who dwell upon it immense material advantages and opportunities. In such a country we live. But I love to think of a glorious nation built upon the will of free men, set apart for the propagation and cultivation of humanity's best ideal of a free government, and made ready for the growth and fruitage of the highest aspirations of patriotism. This is the country that lives in us. I indulge in no mere figure of speech when I say that our nation, the immortal spirit of our domain, lives in us—in our hearts and minds and consciences. There it must find its nutriment or die. This thought more than any other presents to our minds the impressiveness and responsibility of American citizenship. The land we live in seems to be strong and active. But how fares the land that lives in us? Are we sure that we are doing all we ought to keep it in vigor and health? Are we keeping its roots well surrounded by the fertile soil of loving allegiance, and are we furnishing them the invigorating moisture of unselfish fidelity? Are we as diligent as we ought to be to protect this precious growth against the poison that must arise from the decay of harmony and honesty and industry and frugality; and are we sufficiently watchful against the deadly, burrowing pests of consuming greed and cankerous cupidity? Our answers to these questions make up the account of our stewardship as keepers of a sacred trust.

HOLIDAY OBSERVANCE

The land we live in is safe as long as we are dutifully careful of the land that lives in us. But good intentions and fine sentiments will not meet the emergency. If we would bestow upon the land that lives in us the care it needs, it is indispensable that we should recognize the weakness of our human nature, and our susceptibility to temptations and influences that interfere with a full conception of our obligations; and thereupon we should see to it that cupidity and selfishness do not blind our consciences or dull our efforts.

From different points of view I have invited you to consider with me what obligations and responsibilities rest upon those who in this country of ours are entitled to be called good citizens. The things I pointed out may be trite. I know I have spoken in the way of exhortation rather than with an attempt to say something new and striking. Perhaps you have suspected, what I am quite willing to confess, that, behind all that I have said, there is in my mind a sober conviction that we all can and ought to do more for the country that lives in us than it has been our habit to do; and that no better means to this end are at hand than a revival

of pure patriotic affection for our country for
its own sake, and the acceptance, as permanent
occupants in our hearts and minds, of the
virtues which Washington regarded as all that
was necessary to make us a great and happy
people, and which he declared to be "the great
and essential pillars of public felicity"—harmony,
honesty, industry and frugality.